TAGINE RECIPES

Step-by-step Easy recipes to prepare at home for Moroccan one-pot cooking

TABLE OF CONTENTS

MOROCCAN TAGINE OF SHRIMP 6

MOROCCAN CHICKEN TAGINE 8

MOROCCAN LAMB TAGINE 10

MOROCCAN CHICKEN AND APRICOT TAGINE 12

MOROCCAN FISH TAGINE 14

MOROCCAN KEFTA TAGINE 16

MOROCCAN VEGETARIAN TAGINE 18

BEEF TAGINE WITH ARTICHOCKES 20

MOROCCAN SAUSAGE TAGINE 22

FISH TAGINE WITH ALMONDS 24

TAGINE OF LAMB & SAUSAGES 26

VEGETABLE TAGINE 28

LAMB TAGINE 29

MOROCCAN MEATBALL TAGINE 31

CHICKEN TAGINE 33

CRANBERRY TAGINE 35

FRUITY LAMB TAGINE 37

LAMB TAGINE WITH SWEET POTATOES 39

SIMPLE TAGINE 41

CHICKPEA TAGINE 43

MOROCCAN TAGINE 45

LAMB STEW 47

MOROCCAN MUSHROOMS 49

VEGETABLES & CHICKPEAS 51

LAMB WITH DATES 53

LAMB PILAU 55

TAGINE SALADS 58

VEGETABLE TAGINE SALAD 58

TAGINE CHICKEN SALAD 60

LAMB TAGINE SALAD 62

TURKEY TAGINE SALAD 64

GOAT TAGINE SALAD 66

COUSCOUS SALAD 68

DATE TAGINE 69

MOROCCAN TAGINE SALAD 70

MOROCCAN GOAT TAGINE SALAD 71

MOROCCAN TURKEY SALAD 73

MOROCCAN SALAD 74

BEETROOT MOROCCAN SALAD 75

TAKTOUKA 76

BAKOULA SALAD WITH SPINACH 77

Copyright 2019 by Noah Jerris - All rights reserved.

This document is geared towards providing exact and reliable information in regards to the topic and issue covered. The publication is sold with the idea that the publisher is not required to render accounting, officially permitted, or otherwise, qualified services. If advice is necessary, legal or professional, a practiced individual in the profession should be ordered.

- From a Declaration of Principles which was accepted and approved equally by a Committee of the American Bar Association and a Committee of Publishers and Associations.

In no way is it legal to reproduce, duplicate, or transmit any part of this document in either electronic means or in printed format. Recording of this publication is strictly prohibited and any storage of this document is not allowed unless with written permission from the publisher. All rights reserved.

The information provided herein is stated to be truthful and consistent, in that any liability, in terms of inattention or otherwise, by any usage or abuse of any policies, processes, or directions contained within is the solitary and utter responsibility of the recipient reader. Under no circumstances will any legal responsibility or blame be held against the publisher for any reparation, damages, or monetary loss due to the information herein, either directly or indirectly.

Respective authors own all copyrights not held by the publisher.

The information herein is offered for informational purposes solely, and is universal as so. The presentation of the information is without contract or any type of guarantee assurance.

The trademarks that are used are without any consent, and the publication of the trademark is without permission or backing by the trademark owner. All trademarks and brands within this book are for clarifying purposes only and are the owned by the owners themselves, not affiliated with this document.

Introduction

Tagine recipes for personal enjoyment but also for family enjoyment. You will love them for sure for how easy it is to prepare them.

MOROCCAN TAGINE OF SHRIMP

Serves: **6**
Prep Time: **40** Minutes
Cook Time: **60** Minutes
Total Time: **100** Minutes

INGREDIENTS

- 2 lb. shrimp
- 2 lb. tomatoes
- ¼ cup olive oil1
- 1 onion
- 4 cloves garlic
- 1 tsp onion
- 1 tsp paprika
- 1 tsp cumin
- 1 tsp salt
- 1 tsp black pepper
- 1 tsp parsley
- 1 tsp coriander

DIRECTIONS

1. Place the base of the tagine and cook on low heat
2. Add onion, olive oil, garlic and cook for several minutes
3. Add the tomatoes, spices and cook on low heat
4. Simmer for 20-30 minutes, when ready remove from heat and serve

MOROCCAN CHICKEN TAGINE

Serves: **4**

Prep Time: **10** Minutes

Cook Time: **60** Minutes

Total Time: **70** Minutes

INGREDIENTS

- 1 lemon
- 1 chicken
- 2 onions
- 2 garlic cloves
- 1 cilantro
- 1 handful parsley
- 1 tsp ginger
- 1 tsp black pepper
- 1 tsp turmeric
- 1 tsp salt
- ½ cup olive oil
- ½ cup olives
- ½ cup water

DIRECTIONS

1. Place the chicken in a bowl with onion, garlic, cilantro, parsley, ginger, pepper, turmeric, salt and mix well
2. Let the chicken marinate overnight
3. In a tagine add olive oil and add marinated chicken
4. Add olives, lemon and drizzle more olive oil
5. Add water and cook on low heat
6. Cook the chicken on low heat for 1 hour or until tender

MOROCCAN LAMB TAGINE

Serves: **6**

Prep Time: **10** Minutes

Cook Time: **40** Minutes

Total Time: **50** Minutes

INGREDIENTS

- 2 lb. lamb
- 2 onions
- 2 garlic cloves
- 1 tsp salt
- 1 tsp black pepper
- 1 tsp ginger
- 1 tsp turmeric
- ¼ cup olive oil
- 2 cups water
- ½ lb. prunes
- 1 tablespoon honey
- 1 tablespoon sugar
- 1 tsp cinnamon

DIRECTIONS

1. In a bowl combine onion, garlic spices and mix the meat with the onion mixture
2. In a skillet heat olive oil and fry the meat for 3-4 minutes
3. Place the meat mixture into a pressure cooker, add 2 cups of water, cilantro and cook on high heat for 30-40 minutes
4. When the meat is cooked reduce the sauce
5. In a pot add the prunes and cook on low heat with the liquid from the meat
6. Add cinnamon, sugar, honey and simmer on low heat for 10 minutes
7. Place the cooked meat on a plate, spoon the prunes and serve

MOROCCAN CHICKEN AND APRICOT TAGINE

Serves: **6**

Prep Time: **10** Minutes

Cook Time: **60** Minutes

Total Time: **70** Minutes

INGREDIENTS

- 1 chicken
- 2 onion
- 2 garlic cloves
- 1 tsp salt
- 1 tsp ginger
- 1 tsp black pepper
- 1 tsp turmeric
- 2 tablespoons butter
- 1 tablespoon olive oil
- 1 cinnamon stick
- 1 cup water
- 2 tablespoons honey
- 1 cup apricots

DIRECTIONS

1. In a bowl combine all spices and add the chicken
2. Toss to coat
3. In a tagine melt butter and add onions, garlic and the cinnamon stick
4. Add the chicken and top with onions and cilantro
5. Add water and cook for 50-60 minutes
6. In a skillet combine cinnamon, honey and cook on low heat for 5-6 minutes
7. When ready serve the chicken with honey mixture and apricots

MOROCCAN FISH TAGINE

Serves: **4**

Prep Time: **10** Minutes

Cook Time: **60** Minutes

Total Time: **70** Minutes

INGREDIENTS

- 2 lb. fish
- 2 bell peppers
- ¼ cup olive oil
- 1 onion
- 1 carrot
- 2 potatoes
- 1 tsp ginger
- 1 tsp salt
- 1 tsp turmeric
- 2 tomatoes
- 1 lemon

DIRECTIONS

1. Place the chermoula marinade in a bowl
2. Add the fish and refrigerate overnight
3. Heat olive oil in a tagine, add onion, potatoes, turmeric, salt, pepper and top with tomato slices
4. Add the fist to the tagine and top with roasted bell peppers
5. Garnish with lemon slices and cook on low heat for 1 hour or until the fish is done
6. When ready remove from heat and serve

MOROCCAN KEFTA TAGINE

Serves: **4-5**

Prep Time: **10** Minutes

Cook Time: **50** Minutes

Total Time: **60** Minutes

INGREDIENTS

- 4 cups tomato sauce

KEFTA MEATBALLS

- 1 lb. ground beef
- 1 onion
- 1 green pepper
- 1 tsp paprika
- 1 tsp cumin
- 1 tsp salt
- 1 tsp cinnamon
- 1 tsp black pepper
- ¼ cup parsley
- ¼ cup coriander

DIRECTIONS

1. In a bowl combine all ingredients for the meatballs
2. Mix well and form small meatballs
3. In a the cook the tomato sauce on low heat and bring to a simmer
4. Add the meatballs and cook for 40 minutes or until the sauce is thick
5. When ready remove from heat and serve

MOROCCAN VEGETARIAN TAGINE

Serves: **4**

Prep Time: **10** Minutes

Cook Time: **40** Minutes

Total Time: **50** Minutes

INGREDIENTS

- 1 onion
- 2 garlic cloves
- 2 tablespoons olive oil
- 1 tsp salt
- 1 tsp ginger
- 1 tsp turmeric
- 1 tsp black pepper
- 2 tablespoons parsley
- 4 carrots
- 1 cup water
- 2 tablespoons honey
- 1 cup cooked chickpeas

DIRECTIONS

1. In a tagine sauté the onions and garlic
2. Add turmeric, ginger, salt, pepper, parsley, carrot and water
3. Bring to a simmer and cook until the carrots are soft
4. Stir in honey, chickpeas, and cook until the sauce is thick
5. When ready remove from heat and serve

BEEF TAGINE WITH ARTICHOCKES

Serves: *4*

Prep Time: *20* Minutes

Cook Time: *60* Minutes

Total Time: *80* Minutes

INGREDIENTS

- 1 lb. beef
- 1 onion
- 2 garlic cloves
- 1 tsp salt
- 1 tsp ginger
- 1 tsp pepper
- 1 tsp turmeric
- 1 tablespoon parsley
- 1 tablespoon cilantro
- ¼ cup olive oil
- 2 cups water
- 1 lb. peas
- 1 lb. artichoke

DIRECTIONS

1. Heat olive oil in tagine and add onion
2. In a bowl combine meat with onion, garlic, spices and mix well
3. Add the mixture to the tagine
4. Add peas, artichoke, water and cook on low heat
5. When ready garnish with lemon slices and serve

MOROCCAN SAUSAGE TAGINE

Serves: *4*

Prep Time: *10* Minutes

Cook Time: *20* Minutes

Total Time: *30* Minutes

INGREDIENTS

- 8 oz. sausage
- 1 onion
- 2 tomatoes
- 1 tsp salt
- 1 tsp cumin
- ½ cup olives
- 1 tsp black pepper
- 4 eggs

DIRECTIONS

1. **Heat olive oil in a skillet and cook sausage until is done**

2. Add onion, tomatoes, olives, seasoning and cook for another 5-10 minutes
3. Pour the eggs over the sausage
4. Cook until the eggs are done
5. When ready remove from heat and serve

FISH TAGINE WITH ALMONDS

Serves: *2*

Prep Time: *10* Minutes

Cook Time: *40* Minutes

Total Time: *50* Minutes

INGREDIENTS

- 1 tablespoon olive oil
- 1 onion
- 2 cups chicken stock
- 2 garlic cloves
- 1-piece ginger
- 1 green chili
- 1 tsp cumin
- 1 tsp coriander
- 1 tsp cinnamon
- 8-10 cherry tomatoes
- 1 tablespoon honey
- 4 oz. white fish
- ½ cup almonds

DIRECTIONS

1. In a tagine add onion and cook until soft
2. Add garlic, ginger, chili, spices and cook on low heat
3. Add tomatoes, honey, chicken stock and simmer on low heat for 10-12 minutes
4. Add the fish to the tagine and simmer until the fish is cooked
5. When ready serve with almonds

TAGINE OF LAMB & SAUSAGES

Serves: **4**

Prep Time: **1** Hour

Cook Time: **3** Hours

Total Time: **4** Housr

INGREDIENTS

MARINADE
- 1 tablespoon cumin
- 1 tsp chili powder
- 1 red onion
- 2 garlic cloves
- 1 tsp ginger
- 2 oz. olive oil
- 1 tablespoon honey
- 1 tsp parsley
- 1 tsp coriander

TAGINE
- 2 lb. lamb
- 2 tablespoons olive oil
- 2 carrots

- 2 red onion
- 6 oz. prunes
- 4 merguez sausages
- 2 mint sprigs

DIRECTIONS

1. Place all ingredients for the marinade in a blender
2. Blend until smooth and pour into a bowl
3. Place the lamb in the marinade bowl and refrigerate overnight
4. In a tagine heat olive oil and cook the lamb over low heat for 5-10 minutes
5. Add remaining ingredients for the tagine and transfer tagine to the oven
6. Cook for 3-4 hours at 300 F or until the meat is tender
7. When ready remove from the oven and serve

VEGETABLE TAGINE

Serves: *4*

Prep Time: *10* Minutes

Cook Time: *20* Minutes

Total Time: *30* Minutes

INGREDIENTS

- 2 tablespoons olive oil
- 2 onions
- 2 courgettes
- 2 tomatoes
- 1 can chickpea
- 2 tablespoons raisin
- 2 cups vegetables stock
- 1 lb. pea

DIRECTIONS

1. In a tagine fry onion until soft
2. Add spices, courgettes, tomatoes, chickpeas, raisins and remaining ingredients

3. Cover and cook for 15-18 minutes or until the pea is cooked
4. When ready remove from heat and serve

LAMB TAGINE

Serves: **6**

Prep Time: **10** Minutes

Cook Time: **90** Minutes

Total Time: **100** Minutes

INGREDIENTS

- 2 tablespoons olive oil
- 1 onion
- 2 carrots
- 1 lb. lamb
- 2 garlic cloves
- 1 tsp cumin
- 1 tsp ginger
- 1 tsp cinnamon
- 1 tablespoon honey
- ¼ lb. apricot
- 1 butternut squash
- 1 cup vegetable stock

DIRECTIONS

1. In a tagine heat olive oil and sauté onion and carrot for 3-4 minutes
2. Add the lamb, garlic, spices and cook for 5-6 minutes
3. Add honey, apricots, vegetables stock, cover and cook for 50-60 minutes
4. Add squash and cook for another 20-30 minutes or until squash is tender
5. When ready remove from heat and serve

MOROCCAN MEATBALL TAGINE

Serves: *6-8*

Prep Time: *10* Minutes

Cook Time: *30* Minutes

Total Time: *40* Minutes

INGREDIENTS

- 2 onions
- 1 lb. lamb
- 1 tsp. cumin
- 1 tsp cinnamon
- 1 tablespoon olive oil
- 1 tsp parsley
- 1 tsp ginger
- 1 red chili
- 1 lb. lamb stock
- ¼ lb. olives
- 1 tsp coriander

DIRECTIONS

1. In a blender add lamb, spices, parsley and blend until smooth
2. Shape mixture into balls set aside
3. In a tagine heat olive oil and add the lamb stock, olives, onion, and meatballs
4. Simmer for 20 minutes or until the meatballs are cooked
5. When ready remove from heat and serve

CHICKEN TAGINE

Serves: **4**

Prep Time: **10** Minutes

Cook Time: **60** Minutes

Total Time: **70** Minutes

INGREDIENTS

- 2 chicken breasts
- 2 chicken thighs
- 2 tablespoons olive oil
- ½ lb. shallots
- 2 garlic cloves
- 1 tsp cumin
- 1tsp coriander
- 1 cinnamon stick
- 1 tsp chili
- 1 lb. butternut squash
- 2 cups chicken stock
- 1 tablespoon honey

DIRECTIONS

1. Heat olive oil in a tagine and brown the chicken breast, when ready remove and set aside

2. Add shallots, garlic, ginger and cook for 30 seconds
3. Add spices, butternut squash and cook for 1-2 minutes
4. Add the chicken and pour over chicken stock, honey, and simmer for 5-10 minutes
5. Transfer to the oven and cook at 300 F for 40-45 minute or until tender
6. When ready remove from heat and serve

CRANBERRY TAGINE

Serves: **4**

Prep Time: **10** Minutes

Cook Time: **30** Minutes

Total Time: **40** Minutes

INGREDIENTS

- 2 tablespoons olive oil
- 2 red onion
- 1-piece ginger
- 1 lb. pumpkin squash
- 1 tsp cinnamon
- 1 tablespoon honey
- 2 lb. tomato passata
- 2 oz. cranberries
- 1 lb. chickpea
- ½ lb. couscous

DIRECTIONS

1. Heat oil in a tagine and fry onions, ginger, pumpkin and spices
2. Add honey, passata and cranberries

3. Bring to boil and simmer until the pumpkin is tender
4. Add chickpeas, couscous and water
5. Simmer until the chickpea and couscous are cooked
6. When ready remove from heat and serve with almonds

FRUITY LAMB TAGINE

Serves: *6*
Prep Time: *10* Minutes

Cook Time: *90*   Minutes

Total Time: *100*   Minutes

INGREDIENTS

- 2 tablespoons olive oil
- 1 lb. lamb
- 1 onion
- 2 carrots
- 2 garlic cloves
- 1 lb. tomato
- 1 lb. chickpea
- ½ lb. apricot
- 2 cups chicken stock

DIRECTIONS

1. **In a tagine brown the lamb on both sides and set aside**
2. **Add onion, carrots, garlic and cook for 2-3 minutes**
3. **Stir in spices, tomatoes, chickpea, apricots and stock**
4. **Bring to a simmer and return the lamb to the tagine**
5. **Simmer for 10-12 minutes**

6. Transfer the tagine to the oven, cook until the meat is tender at 300 F
7. When ready remove from the oven and serve

LAMB TAGINE WITH SWEET POTATOES

Serves: *4*
Prep Time: *10* Minutes

Cook Time: *30* Minutes

Total Time: *40* Minutes

INGREDIENTS

- 2 tablespoons olive oil
- 2 onions
- 2 tablespoons ginger root
- 3 lb. lamb shoulder
- 2 tsp cumin
- 2 tsp paprika
- 1 tsp cinnamon
- 2 lb. passata
- 2 lb. sweet potato
- 1 lb. date

DIRECTIONS

1. In a tagine sauté onion until soft
2. Add ginger, spices, cinnamon and coot for 2-3 minutes
3. Add passata, water and bring to a boil
4. Simmer for 60-70 minutes
5. Add sweet potatoes and remaining ingredients and cook until potatoes are tender
6. When ready remove from heat and serve

SIMPLE TAGINE

Serves: *4*
Prep Time: *10* Minutes

Cook Time: 25 Minutes

Total Time: 35 Minutes

INGREDIENTS

- 2 carrots
- 2 parsnips
- 2 red onions
- 2 red peppers
- 2 tablespoons olive oil
- 1 tsp cumin
- 1 can tomato
- 1 tsp honey

DIRECTIONS

1. In a tagine fry spice for 1 minute
2. Add tomatoes, honey, apricots, water and simmer for 5-6 minutes
3. Stir in remaining ingredients and cook for another 15-18 minutes
4. When ready remove from heat and serve

CHICKPEA TAGINE

Serves: *4-6*
Prep Time: *10* Minutes
Cook Time: *40* Minutes

Total Time: *50*   Minutes

INGREDIENTS

- 1 lb. shallot
- 1 tablespoon olive oil
- 1 butternut squash
- 1 tsp cinnamon
- 1 tsp ginger
- 2 cups vegetable stock
- 8 prunes
- 1 tsp honey
- 1 red pepper
- 1 tablespoon coriander
- 1 tablespoon mint
- ½ lb. couscous
- 1 lb. chickpea

DIRECTIONS

1. In a tagine add tagine and fry for 1-2 minutes per side
2. Add onion, ginger and cook for another 2 minutes
3. Add water, honey, carrots, seasoning, vegetable stock and bring to a boil

4. Add remaining ingredients and bring to a simmer
5. Cook for 30 minutes or until the chicken is tender
6. When ready remove from heat and serve

MOROCCAN TAGINE

Serves: *4*
Prep Time: *10* Minutes

Cook Time: **50**   Minutes

Total Time: **60**   Minutes

INGREDIENTS

- 2 red onions
- 2 garlic cloves
- 3 oz lemon juice
- 3 oz. olive oil
- 1 tablespoon honey
- 1 tsp coriander

TAGINE

- 1 tablespoon olive oil
- 2 carrots
- 2 parsnips
- 2 red onions
- 2 potatoes
- 2 leeks
- 8 prunes

DIRECTIONS

1. In a blender add all ingredients for the marinade and blend until smooth
2. In a casserole dish drizzle olive oil
3. Add the marinade and pour water and remaining tagine ingredients

4. Bake at 300 F for 40-45 minutes
5. When ready remove from heat and serve

LAMB STEW

Serves: *4*
Prep Time: *10* Minutes
Cook Time: *30* Minutes

Total Time: *40* Minutes

INGREDIENTS

- 2 tablespoons olive oil
- 1 lb. lamb
- 1 onion
- 2 garlic cloves
- 1 tablespoon ginger
- 4 dried apricots
- 1 cup chicken stock

DIRECTIONS

1. **In a tagine heat olive oil and fry meat until brown**
2. **Add onion, ginger, garlic and fry until soft**
3. **Add remaining ingredients simmer for 25-30 minutes**
4. **When ready remove from heat and serve with couscous**

MOROCCAN MUSHROOMS

Serves: *4*

Prep Time: *10* Minutes

Cook Time: *20* Minutes

Total Time: *30* Minutes

INGREDIENTS

- 1 red onion
- 1 tsp olive oil
- 1 tsp cinnamon
- 1 tsp cumin
- 1 lb. mushrooms
- 1 can tomatoes
- 1 can chickpeas
- 1 tsp honey
- ½ lb. couscous

DIRECTIONS

1. In a tagine fry onion until soft
2. Add cumin, cinnamon, mushrooms and cook for 2-3 minutes
3. Add tomatoes, chickpeas, honey and simmer for 8-10 minutes
4. Combine couscous with apricots, seasoning and pour over mushrooms
5. Add remaining ingredients and cook for another 8-10 minutes
6. When ready remove from heat and serve

VEGETABLES & CHICKPEAS

Serves: *4*

Prep Time: *10* Minutes

Cook Time: *50* Minutes

Total Time: *60* Minutes

INGREDIENTS

- 2 courgettes

- 2 garlic cloves
- 2 red peppers
- 2 potatoes
- 1 onion
- 1 tablespoon coriander seeds
- 2 tablespoons olive oil
- 1 can tomatoes
- 1 can chickpeas

DIRECTIONS

1. Roast the vegetables for 40-45 minutes at 200 F
2. When ready remove from the oven and serve
3. Place everything in a tagine and bring to a simmer
4. Add remaining ingredients and cook until vegetables are soft
5. When ready remove from heat and serve

LAMB WITH DATES

Serves: *4*

Prep Time: *10* Minutes

Cook Time: *20* Minutes

Total Time: *30* Minutes

INGREDIENTS

- 1 tablespoon olive oil
- 1 onion
- 1 lb. lamb

- 1 lb. sweet potatoes
- 1 tsp coriander
- 1 tsp cinnamon
- 2 oz. pitted dates
- 1 tablespoon coriander

DIRECTIONS

1. In a tagine fry onion and lamb until brown
2. Add spices, sweet potatoes, water and bring to a boil
3. Bring to a simmer until the lamb is tender
4. When ready remove from heat, sprinkle with coriander and serve

LAMB PILAU

Serves: *4*

Prep Time: *10* Minutes

Cook Time: *15* Minutes

Total Time: *25* Minutes

INGREDIENTS

- **1 tablespoon olive oil**
- **1 onion**
- **1 cinnamon stick**
- **1 lb. lamb fillet**
- **½ lb. basmati rice**

- 1 lamb
- 8 apricots
- mint leaves

DIRECTIONS

1. In a tagine fry onion, cinnamon and lamb until brown
2. Add rice and cook for another 2-3 minutes
3. Add 2 cups water and remaining ingredients and bring to a simmer for 12-15 minutes
4. When ready remove from heat and serve

TAGINE SALADS

VEGETABLE TAGINE SALAD

Serves: **4**

Prep Time: **10** Minutes

Cook Time: **30** Minutes

Total Time: **40** Minutes

INGREDIENTS

- ¼ cooked butternut pumpkin
- 1 carrot
- 1 zucchini
- 1 cup cooked chickpeas
- 1 tablespoon Moroccan seasoning
- ¼ cup olive oil
- 1 cup cooked couscous

- 1 cup cherry tomatoes

DIRECTIONS

1. In a bowl mix all ingredients and mix well
2. Serve with dressing

TAGINE CHICKEN SALAD

Serves: **4**

Prep Time: **10** Minutes

Cook Time: **30** Minutes

Total Time: **40** Minutes

INGREDIENTS

- 1 lb. coocked chicken breast
- 2 tablespoons mayonnaise
- 1 tablespoon lemon juice
- 1 tsp garlic powder
- 1 tsp curry powder
- 1 tsp cinnamon
- 1 tsp paprika
- 1 tsp onion powder
- 1 tsp turmeric
- 1 cup cherry tomatoes

DIRECTIONS

1. In a bowl mix all ingredients and mix well
2. Serve with dressing

LAMB TAGINE SALAD

Serves: **4**

Prep Time: **10** Minutes

Cook Time: **30** Minutes

Total Time: **40** Minutes

INGREDIENTS

- 1 tsp cumin
- 1 tsp coriander
- 1 garlic clove
- 2 tablespoons olive oil
- 1 lb. cooked lamb
- ½ lb. cooked couscous
- 1 carrot
- 2 mint leaves
- 1 tsp coriander
- ¼ cup pomegranate seeds

DIRECTIONS

1. In a bowl mix all ingredients and mix well
2. Serve with dressing

TURKEY TAGINE SALAD

Serves: **4**

Prep Time: **10** Minutes

Cook Time: **30** Minutes

Total Time: **40** Minutes

INGREDIENTS

- 1 tsp cumin
- 1 tsp coriander
- 1 garlic clove
- 2 tablespoons olive oil
- 1 lb. cooked turkey
- ½ lb. cooked chickpeas
- 1 cup cherry tomatoes
- 1 carrot
- 2 mint leaves
- 1 tsp coriander

DIRECTIONS

1. In a bowl mix all ingredients and mix well
2. Serve with dressing

GOAT TAGINE SALAD

Serves: **4**

Prep Time: **10** Minutes

Cook Time: **30** Minutes

Total Time: **40** Minutes

INGREDIENTS

- 1tsp ginger
- 1 tsp black pepper
- 1 tsp turmeric
- 1 lb. goat chunks
- 1 oz. apricots
- 1 tablespoon olive oil
- 1 onion
- 4 garlic cloves
- 1 tablespoon honey
- 1 lb. tomatoes

DIRECTIONS

1. **In a bowl mix all ingredients and mix well**

2. Serve with dressing

COUSCOUS SALAD

Serves: **4**

Prep Time: **10** Minutes

Cook Time: **30** Minutes

Total Time: **40** Minutes

INGREDIENTS

- 1 ½ lb. cooked lamb shoulder
- 2 tablespoons olive oil
- 1 lb. cooked butternut pumpkin
- 1 tablespoon honey
- ½ lb. cooked chickpeas

DIRECTIONS

1. In a bowl mix all ingredients and mix well
2. Serve with dressing

DATE TAGINE

Serves: **4**

Prep Time: **10** Minutes

Cook Time: **30** Minutes

Total Time: **40** Minutes

INGREDIENTS

- 1 tablespoon olive oil
- 1 onion
- 2 cloves garlic
- 1 tsp cumin
- 1 tsp coriander
- 1 tsp ginger
- 1 tsp cinnamon
- 1 can tomatoes
- 2 cups cooked chickpeas
- 1 cup cooked couscous
- 1 cup dates
- 1 cup dates
- ¼ cup lemon juice

DIRECTIONS

1. In a bowl mix all ingredients and mix well
2. Serve with dressing

MOROCCAN TAGINE SALAD

Serves: **4**
Prep Time: **10** Minutes
Cook Time: **30** Minutes
Total Time: **40** Minutes

INGREDIENTS

- 1 lb. cooked chicken thighs
- 8-10 olives
- 1 onion
- 2 garlic cloves
- 1 tablespoon lemon juice
- 1 tsp ground cumin
- 1 tsp coriander
- 1 tomato
- 1 cucumber

DIRECTIONS

1. In a bowl mix all ingredients and mix well
2. Serve with dressing

MOROCCAN GOAT TAGINE SALAD

Serves: **4**
Prep Time: **10** Minutes

Cook Time: **30** Minutes

Total Time: **40** Minutes

INGREDIENTS

- 1 tsp ginger
- 1 tsp black pepper
- 1 tsp turmeric
- 1 lb. cooked shoulder goat
- 2 oz. apricots
- 1 tablespoon olive oil
- 1 onion
- 4-6 garlic cloves
- 1 can tomatoes
- 1 tablespoon honey

DIRECTIONS

1. **In a bowl mix all ingredients and mix well**
2. **Serve with dressing**

MOROCCAN TURKEY SALAD

Serves: **4**

Prep Time: **10** Minutes

Cook Time: **30** Minutes

Total Time: **40** Minutes

INGREDIENTS

- 1 pitta bread
- 1 tablespoon olive oil
- ½ cup tomato
- 1 lb. turkey breast
- 2-3 mint leaves

DIRECTIONS

1. In a bowl mix all ingredients and mix well
2. Serve with dressing

MOROCCAN SALAD

Serves: **4**

Prep Time: **10** Minutes

Cook Time: **30** Minutes

Total Time: **40** Minutes

INGREDIENTS

- 2 avocados
- ½ lb. cherry tomatoes
- 1 cup carrots
- 1 tablespoon lemon juice
- 1 handful almonds
- 1 tablespoon olive oil

DIRECTIONS

1. **In a bowl mix all ingredients and mix well**
2. **Serve with dressing**

BEETROOT MOROCCAN SALAD

Serves: **4**

Prep Time: **10** Minutes

Cook Time: *30*   Minutes

Total Time: *40*   Minutes

INGREDIENTS

- 2 beetroots
- 1 avocado
- 1 shallot
- 1 tsp parsley
- 1 tsp cumin
- 1 tsp lemon juice
- 1 tablespoon wine vinegar

DIRECTIONS

1. In a bowl mix all ingredients and mix well
2. Serve with dressing

TAKTOUKA

Serves: *4*

Prep Time: *10*   Minutes

Cook Time: *30*   Minutes

Total Time: *40*   Minutes

INGREDIENTS

- 2 green peppers
- 2 tablespoons olive oil
- 2 tomatoes
- 1 tsp garlic
- 1 tsp paprika
- 1 tsp parsley
- 1 tsp salt

DIRECTIONS

1. In a bowl mix all ingredients and mix well
2. Serve with dressing

BAKOULA SALAD WITH SPINACH

Serves: **4**

Prep Time: **10** Minutes

Cook Time: **30** Minutes

Total Time: **40** Minutes

INGREDIENTS

- 2 tablespoons olive oil
- ¼ lb. spinach
- ¼ lb. kale leaves
- 2 tablespoons parsley
- 2 tablespoons cilantro
- 1 tablespoon lemon juice
- 1 tsp paprika
- 1 tsp cumin
- 1 handful red olives

DIRECTIONS

1. **In a bowl mix all ingredients and mix well**
2. **Serve with dressing**

THANK YOU FOR READING THIS BOOK!

Printed in Great Britain
by Amazon